PAPER
MAGIC

PAPER MAGIC

CREATING FANTASIES
& PERFORMING TRICKS
WITH PAPER

BY ORMOND McGILL

DRAWINGS BY
ANNE CANEVARI GREEN

THE MILLBROOK PRESS • BROOKFIELD, CONNECTICUT

Library of Congress Cataloging-in-Publication Data

McGill, Ormond.
Paper magic : creating fantasies and performing tricks with paper
/ by Ormond McGill.
p. cm.
Includes bibliographical references and index.
Summary: Step-by-step instructions for performing magic tricks
using paper.
ISBN 1-56294-136-4
1. Paper work—Juvenile literature.   2. Magic—Juvenile
literature. [1. Paper work.   2. Magic tricks.]   I. Title.
TT870.M35   1992
793.8—dc20   91-20996   CIP   AC

CONTENTS

PAPER
MAGIC

FROM ONE MAGICIAN
TO ANOTHER

Magic cast its spell on me at an early age. I practiced tricks, and I learned more and more, until one day I became a magician. Magic is now my way of life, and a wonderful life it is.

Magic is for children of all ages, from one to one hundred. Each of us has a magician hidden deep inside waiting to appear. All we need to do to bring out the magician is learn the secrets of the trade.

I have performed a lot of magic in my life. I will now share my secrets with you. If you follow my instructions carefully and patiently, you can become a magician too.

In the first part of this book, I will show you how to make an assortment of clever paper fantasies. Some are beautiful. Some are interesting. All are fantastic fun. In the second half, I will show you how to perform mystifying magic tricks.

These are a great surprise since paper seems so ordinary and so simple. Paper is all around you just for the picking up. The fun you receive in return is endless.

Magic is a joy to watch and to do. It broadens the horizons of all who learn the art. Show your friends what you have learned. Let them in on the secrets of your trade. Magic is for everyone.

ORMOND MCGILL

PAPER
FANTASIES

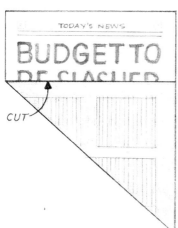

CUT

This paper fantasy is a favorite of mine. Here is how you make a great big shaggy paper tree.

Lay four pages of newspaper folded in half on top of each other. Now, cut about a 12-inch square section out of all the sheets at the same time. Separate the sheets and you have eight 12-inch squares of newspaper.

A tip on making a square from a rectangle: Fold one of the long edges over to the opposite side to make a triangle. Snip off the extra strip of paper. See figure 1.

FIGURE 1

FIGURE 2

FIGURE 3

Next, lay one of the sheets out flat on the table and roll it into a tube. When about 3 inches are left unrolled, add another sheet and keep on rolling. Add a third sheet, tapping the ends as you go to keep the roll even. Keep adding sheets in the same way until you have made one big roll of all eight of the sheets. See figure 2.

Tape or glue the last sheet of paper to the roll. Take a pair of scissors and insert one point into the center of one end of the roll. Make a deep cut halfway down the roll. Make two more cuts of equal length, so that you have made three cuts in all, at equal distances around the roll. See figure 3.

If you don't have very sharp, long scissors, you may have trouble making the cuts. If so, slide the point of the scissors between the layers and cut into the outer layers first, then cut the inner ones.

The three deep scissor cuts create three flaps out of the top half of the roll of paper. Spread these out, as shown in figure 4.

Now, pull up on the three flaps from the center of the roll. Keep pulling stead-

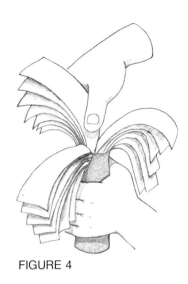

FIGURE 4

ily upward. You will end up with a splendid paper tree.

If you want to make a smaller paper tree, you can use magazine pages instead. If you have some lightweight colored paper, try making a tree out of that. Play with different colors and sizes and amounts of paper. Or, make an enchanted forest!

JACOB'S LADDER

Tell your friends that you will now make a ladder to climb to the top of your Shaggy Tree.

Start by rolling up sheets of newspaper as you did for your Shaggy Tree. Tape or glue the outside edge of the roll. Flatten out the roll and cut about a 4-inch section from its center, as shown in figure 1.

If you find it hard to cut through a roll of eight sheets, you can use fewer sheets. You can still create a ladder, even if it is not quite as tall. You can even make a cute small ladder if you use a half dozen magazine pages instead. The important thing is to cut out the center section of the roll.

When you have cut it out, grasp the two ends of the roll in one hand. See figure 2.

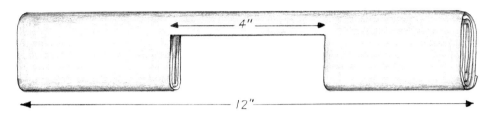

FIGURE 1

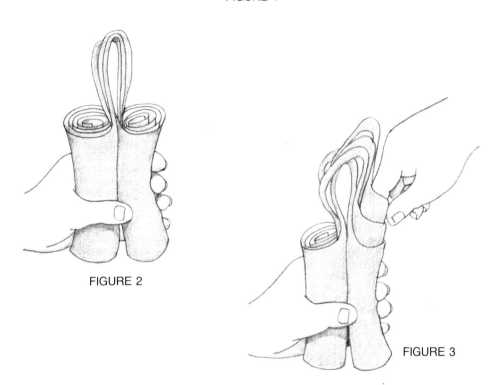

FIGURE 2

FIGURE 3

To make the ladder, start by pulling the rolled paper up about 3 inches from the top of one of the rolls. See figure 3.

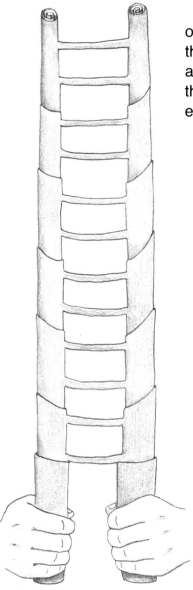

Then, pull up the rolled paper in the other roll until it is at the same height as the first one. Keep pulling the paper up alternately from the top of both rolls until they will go no further. Take one roll in each hand and separate them.

Abracadabra—Jacob's Ladder!

WHIRLIGIG
AND POPPER

Here are two fun things to make in a jiffy with paper. The Whirligig twirls and the Popper goes off with a bang!

To make a Whirligig, cut a paper strip about 8 inches long and 1 inch wide. Then, make two scissor cuts on opposite sides of the strip, cutting halfway through the strip about an inch from its ends. See figure 1.

Loop the strip around and fit the cuts into each other, as shown in figure 2. And there's your Whirligig.

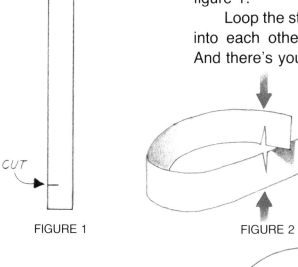

CUT

CUT

FIGURE 1   FIGURE 2

Toss it as high as you can into the air, and it will whirl as it flutters down to the ground.

To make a Popper, take a large square of paper. Any size will do—the larger it is the more noise it will make.

Fold the square in half, as shown in figure 3a, to make a triangle. Open it up, and fold it the other way, as shown in figure 3b. Crease it well.

Now, fold this creased paper square in half, as shown in figure 4a. Push in the end triangles of the folded square to make the Popper. See figure 4b.

Firmly grip one of the points at the base of the folded triangle. Slide your forefinger between the folds so you can hold on as you swing your hand down with a rapid SNAP!

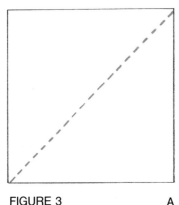
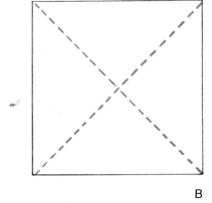

FIGURE 3   A   B

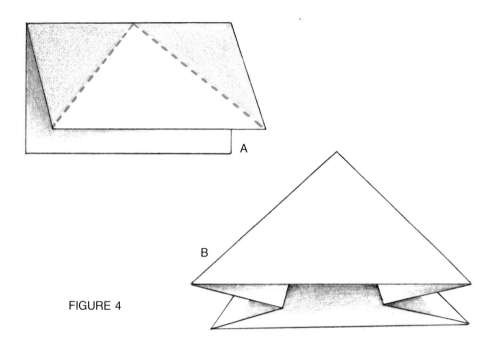

A

B

FIGURE 4

POP

BOUNCING
BUNNY

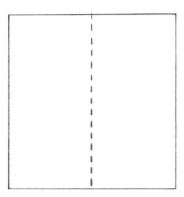

With a few folds and a couple of cuts with the scissors, you'll have a rabbit that will hop when your Popper pops.

Take a square sheet of paper (any size will do) and fold the paper in half lengthwise, right to left, as shown in figure 1.

Now, fold down the top half of the folded paper to make a triangle. See figure 2.

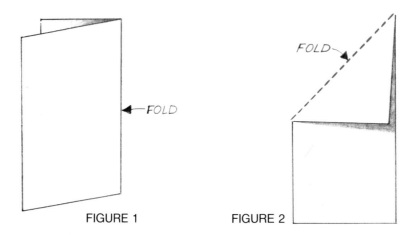

FIGURE 1

FIGURE 2

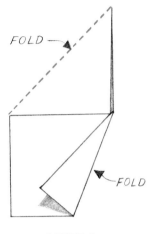

FIGURE 3

On the lower half of the folded paper, fold in an elongated triangle, folding from right to left, as shown in figure 3.

Next, fold the paper up from the middle, so that the bottom half is even with the top half. See figure 4.

Then, lightly sketch the outline of the rabbit's ears and head, and draw a couple of notches for its eyes and nose. Cut along your lines.

Presto! Mr. Rabbit.

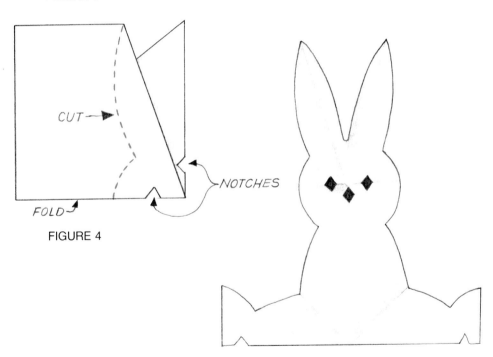

FIGURE 4

MARINER'S WHEEL
AND SNOWFLAKE

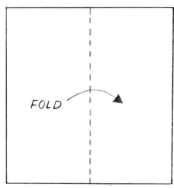

FIGURE 1   A

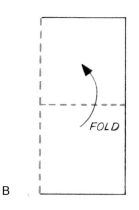

B

With a little bit of know-how, you can take a sheet of ordinary paper, make a few folds, and snip, snip, snip the paper into some lovely, intricate shapes.

To make the Mariner's Wheel and the Snowflake, you need two squares of white paper. The larger the paper, the more spectacular the designs will be.

Let's start with the Mariner's Wheel. Fold the square of paper twice square, that is, once from left to right and another time from top to bottom. See figure 1a,b. Then, fold the paper diagonally. Pay attention to how you fold the paper. Fold the single sheets on top of each other and the folded sheets together, as shown in figure 1c.

Now, fold the triangle in half again, as shown in figure 1d. This time, bring the fold up, and at the same time flip the triangle to the right, so that the four folded

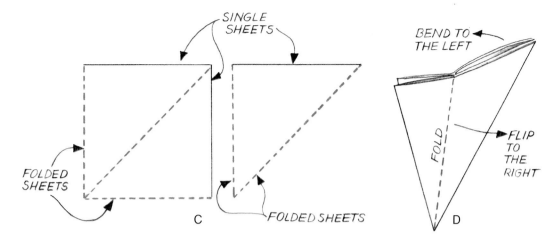

SINGLE SHEETS

FOLDED SHEETS

FOLDED SHEETS

C

BEND TO THE LEFT

FOLD

FLIP TO THE RIGHT

D

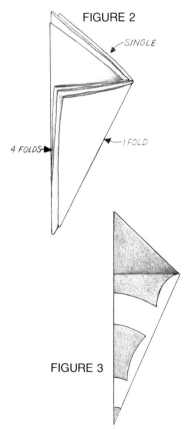

FIGURE 2

SINGLE

4 FOLDS

1 FOLD

FIGURE 3

sheets come together on the left side. The lower right side should be 1 single fold. See figure 2.

With a pencil, lightly mark off the shapes you are going to cut from the paper. The white portion in figure 3 shows the part of the paper you will save. The shaded part is what you will cut away.

When you have finished, open up the paper, and the Mariner's Wheel will unfold.

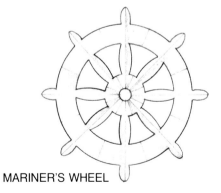

MARINER'S WHEEL

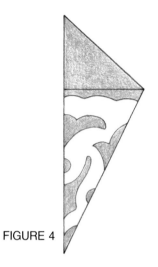

FIGURE 4

You create the Snowflake in exactly the same way, only you cut a different design in the folded paper. Figure 4 shows you the pattern. Figure 5 shows the completed design.

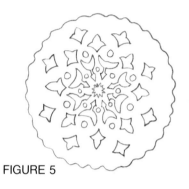

FIGURE 5

The only limit to the number of patterns you create is your imagination. Try displaying them against colored sheets of paper. Figure 6 shows an intricate design against a black background.

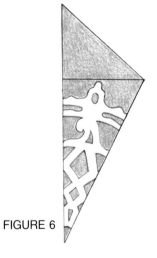

FIGURE 6

▪ 26

SHIP'S
LANTERN

Here's a nice number to complete your repertoire of Paper Fantasies.

To make a lantern, take a square sheet of colored paper and fold it in half diagonally. See figure 1a. Then, fold the triangular shape in half two more times, as shown in figures 1b,c.

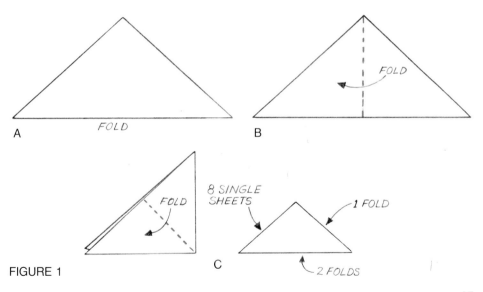

A   *FOLD*

B   *FOLD*

C

FOLD

8 SINGLE SHEETS

1 FOLD

2 FOLDS

FIGURE 1

FIGURE 2

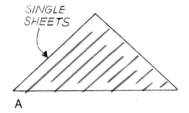

SINGLE SHEETS

A

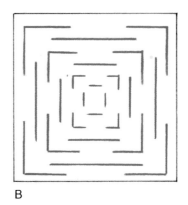

B

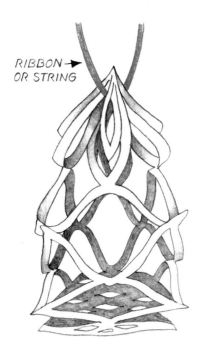

RIBBON → OR STRING

Now, take this folded triangle of paper and cut into the two folded edges of the paper, first from one side and then from the other, as shown in figure 2a. Do not cut all the way across the triangle! Leave about half an inch of folded paper intact. After you've made your cuts, unfold the paper, as in figure 2b.

Bring the four outer corners of the paper together and tape or glue them in place. Then, gently pull the center of the paper down to make a Ship's Lantern.

Next, thread a ribbon or rope through the top of your lantern and hang it from a hook or swing it in your hand. Can you see the lantern, lighting the way for the ship's captain as he paces the deck at night?

DIAMOND
THIEVES

Storytelling can be magical in itself. But when you add paper magic to your tale, the story will become such a puzzle that you may even surprise yourself! To be most effective, you should learn the story by heart and practice the magic trick several times in secret before you set out to dazzle your audience.

Here is what you say and what you AP-PEAR to do:

This is a story about two thieves and the valuable diamonds they tried to steal. I will tear up this napkin and form seven pellets. Tear the napkin and roll each piece up tightly into a little ball. Place the balls in a row on the table.

These little paper balls represent the characters in the story. Two of them are the thieves. The rest are diamonds. I will place the two thieves to one side. Pick up two of the pellets and place them to one side.

My two hands represent the safes where the diamonds are kept under lock and key at night. Show your hands.

I am the security guard who protects the diamonds. But somehow both of the thieves sneaked by me and each of them crawled secretly inside a safe. Place one thief pellet in each of your hands. The other pellets remain in a row on the table. See figure 1.

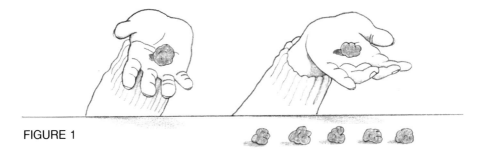

FIGURE 1

I picked up the diamonds that evening to place them in their safes. Pick up the pellets alternately with each hand, starting with your right hand. See figure 2.

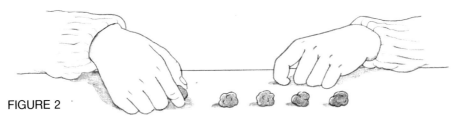

FIGURE 2

For some reason, I felt nervous, so I took the diamonds back out of the safes to make sure they were all there. Replace the diamonds in a row on the table, dropping them alternately from each hand.

They were all there; so I picked them up as before and returned them to their safes. Pick up the diamonds alternately, as before.

What I didn't know was that a thief was inside each safe along with the diamonds. A robbery was about to take place! But I am a magician who protects the diamonds with my magic powers!

The next morning, when I opened the safes, guess what I found! All the diamonds were locked into one of the safes, while the two thieves were locked up in the other. Open your hands and show your surprise. The two thieves will be in one hand, and the five diamonds will lie in the other. See figure 3.

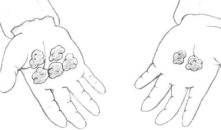

FIGURE 3

Here's what you REALLY do:

Go back to the beginning of the story. You have placed one pellet in each hand to represent the thieves. The spectators tend to overlook the fact that you are using five pellets to represent the diamonds. So, when you pick them up alternately, beginning with your right hand, while it seems that you are picking up an equal number in each hand, you really end up with four pellets in your right hand and three in your left.

When the security guard takes the diamonds from the safes to make sure they're all there, you replace the pellets alternately in a row on the table. But, as you replace them, start with your left hand, taking one pellet from the left, one from the right, one from the left, one from the right, one from the left.

All five pellets are now in a row on the table. Without the spectators knowing it, you have put three pellets from your left hand on the table, but only two from your right hand. This leaves two pellets concealed in your right hand.

Once again, pick up the pellets alternately, but this time start with your right hand. So, you pick up one pellet with your right hand, one with your left, one with your right, one with your left, one with your right.

The trick is complete. All you have to do is conclude the story. When you open your hands, show how the two pellets, the thieves, are safely captured in your left hand, while all five of the other pellets, the diamonds, are safe in your right hand, as shown in figure 3.

Do you see how the trick works? Now try it on your friends.

A TWISTED
TALE

This is a classic. It fools the best of 'em.

Here's what you APPEAR to do:

You hold up three large paper bands. You made them by cutting strips from a double page of newspaper and pasting or taping the ends of the strips together to form circular bands.

Now, you cut one of the bands in half lengthwise. The result, as expected, is two separate bands. You cut the second band in the same way. This time, instead of two separate bands, you get two bands linked together. Then, you cut the third band in half. Magic! It comes out as one giant band, twice the size of the original one.

Here's what you REALLY do:

You cut the strips from the newspaper. They can be as wide as you want. When you make the bands, you paste the ends together in the following way:

- Band No. 1 Fasten the two ends together with no turns or twists. See figure 1a.
- Band No. 2 Make a half-turn or twist in the band before you fasten the ends together. See figure 1b.
- Band No. 3 Give one end a full turn or twist before fastening the ends together. See figure 1c.

You are now ready to perform. It's easy! Simply cut each band in half lengthwise. Surprising things will happen:
- Band No. 1 will turn into two separate bands.
- Band No. 2 will turn into one large, double-sized band.
- Band No. 3 will turn into two bands linked together.

FIGURE 1

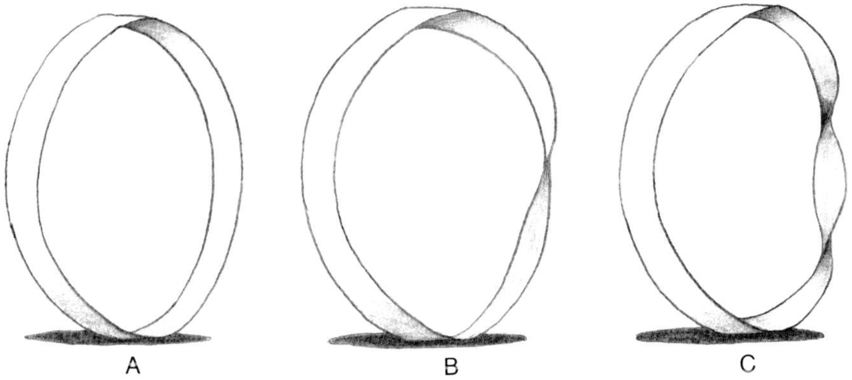

A

B

C

IT MUST BE
MINDREADING

To do this trick you'll need to make five discs and five cards out of stiff paper or cardboard. The circles, or discs, should be about 2 inches across, and the cards should be about 2 inches square.

Each disc has four magic numbers on it. Write them on your five discs with a felt-tipped pen, following the instructions exactly as shown in figure 1.

Write these four same magic numbers on each of the five square cards. They are matching sets. They are all you need to read your spectators' minds.

Here is what you APPEAR to do:

Lay out the cards on the table and place the discs with matching numbers on top of them. Show your audience that the numbers match. Then, gather up the cards and give them to a spectator to shuffle together. Gather up the discs yourself, stack them number side down,

SECRET
5-NUMBER DISC

FIGURE 1

■ 39

and cover them with a handkerchief or napkin.

Tell the spectator to select one of the numbered cards from the stack. Then tell him or her to concentrate very hard on the numbers on his card. Explain that you will now read his or her mind and select from under the handkerchief the disc with the numbers that match those on the spectator's card. Reach beneath the handkerchief and bring out a disc. The spectator names his or her numbers. You show that the number on the disc you hold is a match! It Must Be Mind-reading!

Here's what you REALLY do:

Unknown to the spectators, you have a secret disc. This disc has five numbers on it: 3 8 5 2 4. You place this secret disc in your pocket or on your lap along with a handkerchief. Now, you're ready to do the trick.

Show the five numbered discs and cards. Place them in a row on the table so everyone can see that the numbers match. Then, gather up the cards and give the stack to the spectator, who mixes them up and selects one.

While the spectator is concentrating on the numbers on the card he or she has chosen, you gather up the discs and turn them number side down. In this process, you reach in your pocket and palm the secret disc. Bring it out concealed in your hand along with the handkerchief. As you stack up the discs you secretly add the 5-number disc on top of the stack, and then cover the stack with the handkerchief.

When the spectator is done concentrating, you reach under the handkerchief, fumble around a bit as though trying to figure out which disc you should bring out. Then, bring out the secret disc you added to the top of the stack. When the person names the number on his or her card, all you have to do is casually turn the disc you hold to conceal the one number that does not correspond to the four numbers on the spectator's card. See figure 2.

In this way, you can show whatever numbers the spectator names, by simply hiding the extra number with your thumb. You'll get lots of practice in mindreading because your friends will ask you to do this trick over and over again.

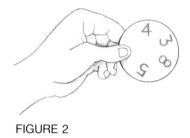

FIGURE 2

CHINESE
COMPASS

This magic compass behaves unlike any compass you have ever seen.

To make one, begin by cutting a square piece of cardboard into an octagon, or an eight-sided shape. Use a ruler to carefully measure off a 3-inch square.

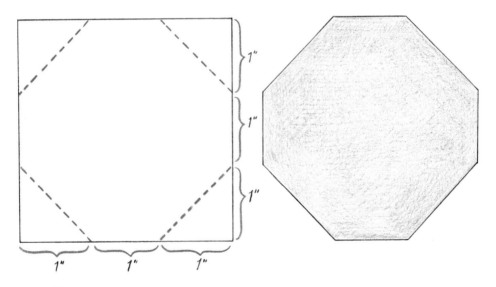

FIGURE 1

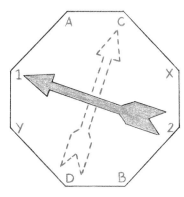

FIGURE 2

Now, place pen marks on each side of the square, dividing them into three even sections, 1 inch each. Then, draw diagonal lines from one side to another, as shown in figure 1. Cut along these lines to trim off the four corners. You'll end up with an eight-sided compass.

Draw an arrow crosswise on the compass, as shown in figure 2. Draw an identical arrow on the opposite side at right angles to the first arrow, as illustrated by the dotted lines in figure 2. Copy the letters and numbers onto your compass exactly as shown in figure 2.

Here is what you APPEAR to do:

The arrow on the compass seems to move about and point in various directions in the most mysterious way. You will find your magic baffles your friends. And even when you show them how to do it, you and your friends may still wonder why it works.

Here is what you REALLY do:

Grip the Chinese Compass in your left hand at points A and B, as shown in figure 3a. Now, place the tip of your right forefinger under the right side of the compass and flip the compass over from right

FIGURE 3

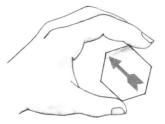

COMPASS HELD IN
A-B POSITION

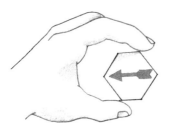

COMPASS HELD IN
C-D POSITION

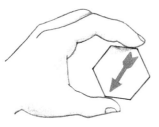

COMPASS HELD IN
X-Y POSITION

to left. It will appear that the arrows on both sides point in the same direction. Keep spinning the compass to give the spectators a good look at the arrows.

Now, shift your hold on the compass to points C and D, as shown in figure 3b. Flip the compass as you did before, by lifting up from underneath its right side with your right forefinger. The arrows on each side will appear to point at right angles to each other. Impress your audience with the position of the arrows by flipping the compass over several times.

Next, shift your left fingers to the points X and Y. See figure 3c. This time, when you spin the compass from right to left, the arrows on each side will seem to point in opposite directions.

To complete the magic, hold the compass as you did at first, as in figure 3a. The arrows will once again point in the same direction.

Here is the story you tell as you follow the sequence of the shifting arrows:

Have you ever seen a Chinese Compass? Well, I'll show you one. It's very useful because it has two arrows, one on top and one underneath. You will notice (flip it over, as in figure 3a) *that the arrows always point in the same direction.*

(Shift to the 3b position.) *But, of course, if the Chinese wish to go due East* (show compass pointing to the left), *they have to steer due North!* (Flip the compass over and the underside arrow comes up pointing at a right angle.)

But, it has one very great advantage over other compasses. (Flip the compass face up once more and shift to the 3c position.) *It shows them not only where they are going* (flip the compass over), *it shows them where they have been!*

SLYDINI'S
DANCE

This trick, created by the nimble-fingered magician, Slydini, is a lesson in misdirection. It has long been a favorite of magicians. With practice, you'll be able to perform it as smoothly as a dance.

Here's what you APPEAR to do:

You use an empty tissue box, with the top cut off, and four tissues. You perform the trick while seated behind a table, with the empty box on one side of the table. You roll each tissue into a ball, and through a series of motions, one by one, the paper balls disappear from your hands and assemble in the box.

Here's what you REALLY do:

Position yourself behind the table with the four paper balls in front of you and to your right. The empty tissue box is on the left side of the table.

Show your audience your empty hands. Pick up one of the paper balls and wave it over the box. Now, turn your body to the left so that your right side is facing the audience. Bring your hands up to shoulder height and roll the paper ball between your hands.

Then, close your left hand around the ball and point to your left fist with your right hand. Open your left hand to show that the ball is still there. Pick up the ball from your left hand with the fingers of your right hand. Slowly lower and raise the ball several more times above the box, making sure that the audience knows that you have not slipped the ball into the box. Return the paper ball to the position between your palms and roll it even tighter.

Now, move your right hand away from your left, closing the left as if it held the ball, but really keeping it concealed, or palmed, in your right hand. You'll have to practice palming the ball, so that your audience doesn't in the least suspect that you have something tucked away in your palm when you show them the back of your hand. See figure 1.

Raise your left fist and turn your hand over so that your thumb points downward and your palm is away from the spectators. Simultaneously lower your right hand to rest gently on the edge of

FIGURE 1

the table and drop the palmed ball into your lap. Bring your left hand toward the box and, at the same time, bring your right hand up to the left. Both hands are held some distance over the box.

Use your right hand to pry open the fingers of your left hand, so the spectators can see that each hand is empty. However, you pretend to act as though you were still holding the ball (although it is now invisible), and you pretend to drop the imaginary ball into the box.

Now, bend forward and look into the box, saying, "Yes, I have magic in there, alright!" This is amusing to the audience because they can see that your hands are empty. Actually the ball is lying in your lap.

Pick up the second paper ball and exhibit it in your left hand while your right hand casually drops to your lap to palm the first ball. When doing this, take care to keep the back of your hands toward the spectators, so the ball remains out of sight.

Place your hands together, pushing the visible ball to your fingertips while the hidden ball remains squeezed in your palm, as shown in figure 2.

Turn back to the front position, raise the visible ball to your lips, and blow on

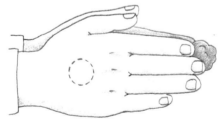

FIGURE 2

it. This gives you an opportunity to palm the hidden ball in your right hand.

As soon as the paper ball is palmed, separate your hands. Drop your right hand a few inches, then reach up and touch the second ball with your fingertips. Then, as if to remind the audience that this ball is to go into the box, reach out with your right hand and dip it into the box. In this motion, secretly drop the palmed ball into the box. Perform the same action again, making certain that this time the spectators are certain that your right hand is empty.

The ruse of secretly loading the ball into the box is very deceptive. Remember that the audience did not know that the first ball was in your lap, nor did they see you drop the first ball into the box while you were handling the second ball.

After you have indicated that the second ball is to go into the box, handle it exactly as you did the first ball. In other words, drop it secretly into your lap and pretend to make it disappear while holding your hands over the box.

Go through the same procedure with the third and fourth paper balls.

By this time, the audience is fully aware that you wish them to believe that the three paper balls have simply vanished and passed invisibly into the box. Actually, you have secretly put three balls into the box, and one ball is on your lap. You must now get this last ball into the box to join the three other balls. To do so, follow these instructions:

Pretend to pick an imaginary paper ball from the air and put it in your left hand. Close your hand as if it actually contained the ball. Carefully open your left hand and feign surprise that nothing is there. Look up into the air and make a grab with your left hand. During this action, your right hand drops to your lap and palms the fourth ball. Then, drop the fourth ball into the box, in the same way that you dropped the first three.

Open your left hand and show it empty. Also show your right hand empty. Finally, deliberately pick up the box and tilt it toward the audience, spilling out the four paper balls. They will gasp in wonder!

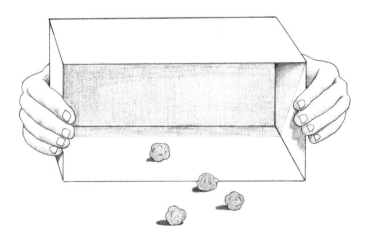

TORN AND
RESTORED

This trick is really two tricks in one. It's a trick for a master magician. Practice hard, and you'll become one yourself.

Here's what you APPEAR to do:

First you show a paper napkin and tear it into pieces. You roll the pieces into a ball, then open the ball, and the torn napkin is magically restored to one piece. But that's just half the fun! Then you offer to give your audience a lesson in magic and tell them how the trick is done.

You tell them you actually use two napkins, one that you palm in your left hand. You demonstrate this by rolling the napkin into a ball and concealing, or palming, it in your left hand. You take another napkin, tear it into bits, roll it into a ball, and show how you secretly exchanged the ball of torn pieces for the balled-up whole napkin. When opened, of course, there is the whole napkin. But what to do with the torn pieces now palmed in your left hand? Now comes the magical finale. You touch these torn pieces with a pencil, your magic wand, open up the ball, and that napkin has also been restored!

Here's how you REALLY do it:

Arrange two paper napkins on the right side of the table. Place two duplicate paper napkins rolled tightly into balls between the corners of each napkin. See figure 1. Note how the napkins are folded to conceal the balled duplicate napkins.

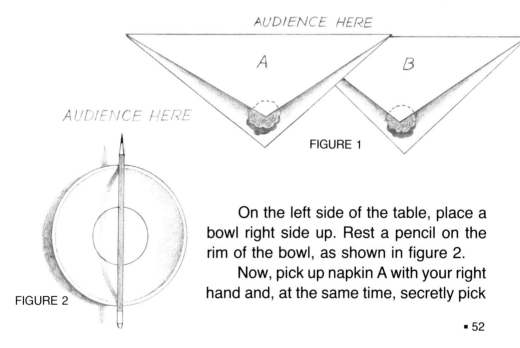

AUDIENCE HERE

A   B

AUDIENCE HERE

FIGURE 1

FIGURE 2

On the left side of the table, place a bowl right side up. Rest a pencil on the rim of the bowl, as shown in figure 2.

Now, pick up napkin A with your right hand and, at the same time, secretly pick

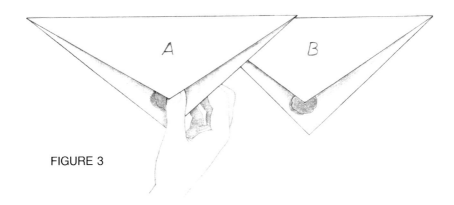

FIGURE 3

up the concealed ball by palming it into your right hand. See figure 3.

The audience must never know you have this ball, or that you use more than one napkin in the trick. Not yet.

You can show the displayed napkin freely on both sides. Meanwhile, the ball is palmed in your right hand, as shown in figure 4.

PALMED BALL

FIGURE 4

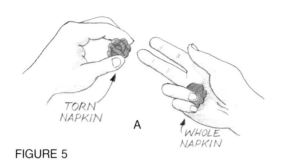

TORN
NAPKIN

A

WHOLE
NAPKIN

FIGURE 5

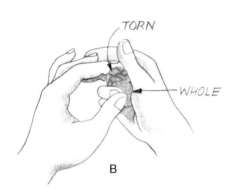

TORN

WHOLE

B

Now, tear the napkin into pieces, roll the pieces into a ball, and hold them in your left hand. See figure 5a. Bring your hands together and place both balls in your left hand. Make sure you have put the torn ball in front of the secret whole one. See figure 5b. Now pick up both balls squeezed together so that they look like one ball. The audience will be no wiser. See figure 5c.

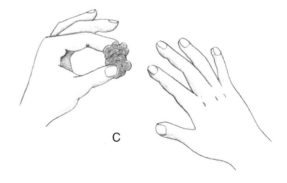

C

Hold your hands with your palms toward the audience so they see they are empty, and it appears you are simply holding the ball of torn pieces of napkin.

Now, place your right hand casually over the balls, and palm away the ball of torn pieces, which is on top. This is easy to do, since the audience is watching one ball while you secretly steal away the other one. They thought you had only one ball in the first place.

Then, reach over to the left side of the table and take the pencil from the bowl with your right hand. As you do this, secretly drop the palmed ball into the bowl. See figure 6.

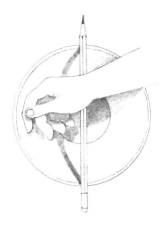

FIGURE 6

Tell your audience, "I will use this pencil as a magic wand." Touch the ball displayed in your left fingers with your wand and return it to rest on the brim of the bowl.

Your hands are empty now, so all you have to do is unroll the napkin and show that it has been magically restored. The first part of the trick is over.

Now for the second part, where you *apparently* show your audience how the trick is done.

You explain, "I really used two napkins, duplicates of each other, to do the trick. One was rolled up in a tight ball like this." (We'll call this napkin B.) Roll up the napkin you have just "restored," and show how you palmed it in your left hand. Then say, "I showed you only one napkin."

Pick up a third napkin. (We'll call this napkin A.) At the same time, secretly palm a duplicate ball, which you have concealed in your lap, in your right hand. (We'll call this napkin C.) The audience must not know you have this extra balled napkin concealed in your right hand.

You hold napkin A up for display. But this time, you have a balled napkin palmed in your left hand that the audience knows about, and another one, secretly palmed in your right hand. See figure 7.

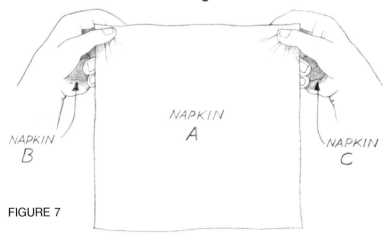

NAPKIN
A

NAPKIN
B

NAPKIN
C

FIGURE 7

■ 56

The trick now continues as it did in the first show. You tear the napkin and roll it into a ball. But this time, you hold both napkins B and C together with the pieces you have just torn, napkin A, in your left hand. The whole napkin is in front. Show these to the audience. The audience thinks you have one ball of torn pieces and one ball of whole napkin. Then, reach over and palm off the torn pieces into your right hand. This move will not be noticed because the audience still sees the two balls in your left hand displayed before them.

At this time, reach over for your pencil with your right hand and drop the torn pieces secretly into the bowl. You are ready for the surprise finale of the trick.

You admit to your audience, "The pencil is really just a pretend wand. Everyone watch and see how I switch the torn pieces for the whole napkin in my hand."

As you say this, touch the pencil to your left hand and let the audience see how you drop the top ball into the bowl. The audience thinks this is the torn napkin. Go ahead with your explanation, opening out the whole napkin to show how it was restored.

Then wave your wand, saying, "But goodness, ladies and gentlemen, how are we going to get rid of these torn pieces? Well, maybe the best way is just to perform a little more magic." Take the napkin from the bowl, unroll it, and show that this one has also been restored.

As a finishing touch, you might add, "Please keep our secret. Don't tell anyone how we did the Torn and Restored trick."

A LAST WORD

I have given you Paper Magic to set you on the road to becoming a magician yourself.

Aside from the fun of learning a craft, I have learned some things about myself along the way. Magic has built my self-confidence. It has taught me how to share my skills with others. It has brought me many new friendships.

And most of all, it has taught me to believe in vast realms of mysteries just waiting to be explored.

MORE FUN
WITH PAPER

Brown, James C. *Papercrafts for All Seasons.* Belmont, California: Fearon Teaching Aids, 1984.

Curtis, A., and Hindley, J. *The KnowHow Book of Paper Fun: Lots of Things to Make from Paper & Card.* Tulsa: EDC Publishing, 1977.

Lewis, Shari, and Lillian Oppenheimer. *Folding Paper Puppets.* Chelsea, Michigan: Scarborough House, 1962.

Simon, Seymour. *Paper Airplane Book.* New York: Viking Penguin, 1976.

Temko, Florence. *Paper Tricks.* Illustrated by Linda Winchester. New York: Scholastic, Inc., 1988.

INDEX